Siddhartha Gautama
The Buddha

Lisa Zamosky

Publishing Credits

Content Consultant
Radhika Srinivasan

Associate Editor
Christina Hill, M.A.

Assistant Editor
Torrey Maloof

Editorial Assistants
Deborah Buchanan
Kathryn R. Kiley
Judy Tan

Editorial Director
Emily R. Smith, M.A.Ed.

Editor-in-Chief
Sharon Coan, M.S.Ed.

Editorial Manager
Gisela Lee, M.A.

Creative Director
Lee Aucoin

Cover Designer
Lesley Palmer

Designers
Deb Brown
Zac Calbert
Amy Couch
Robin Erickson
Neri Garcia

Publisher
Rachelle Cracchiolo, M.S.Ed.

Teacher Created Materials
5301 Oceanus Drive
Huntington Beach, CA 92649
http://www.tcmpub.com
ISBN 978-0-7439-0431-5

Table of Contents

Buddha Is Born

Siddhartha Gautama (sihd-DAHR-tuh GAU-tuh-muh) was the son of a king. The king's name was Suddhodana (sudd-WHO-dan-ah). This king ruled a tribe called the Shakyas (shak-YAHS).

Gautama would one day become known as The Buddha. He would be the founder of the religion called Buddhism (BOO-dih-zuhm). It took him a long time to find his place in the world. He saw suffering around him. And, he wanted to find ways to help people. From this desire, the world's fourth largest religion was formed.

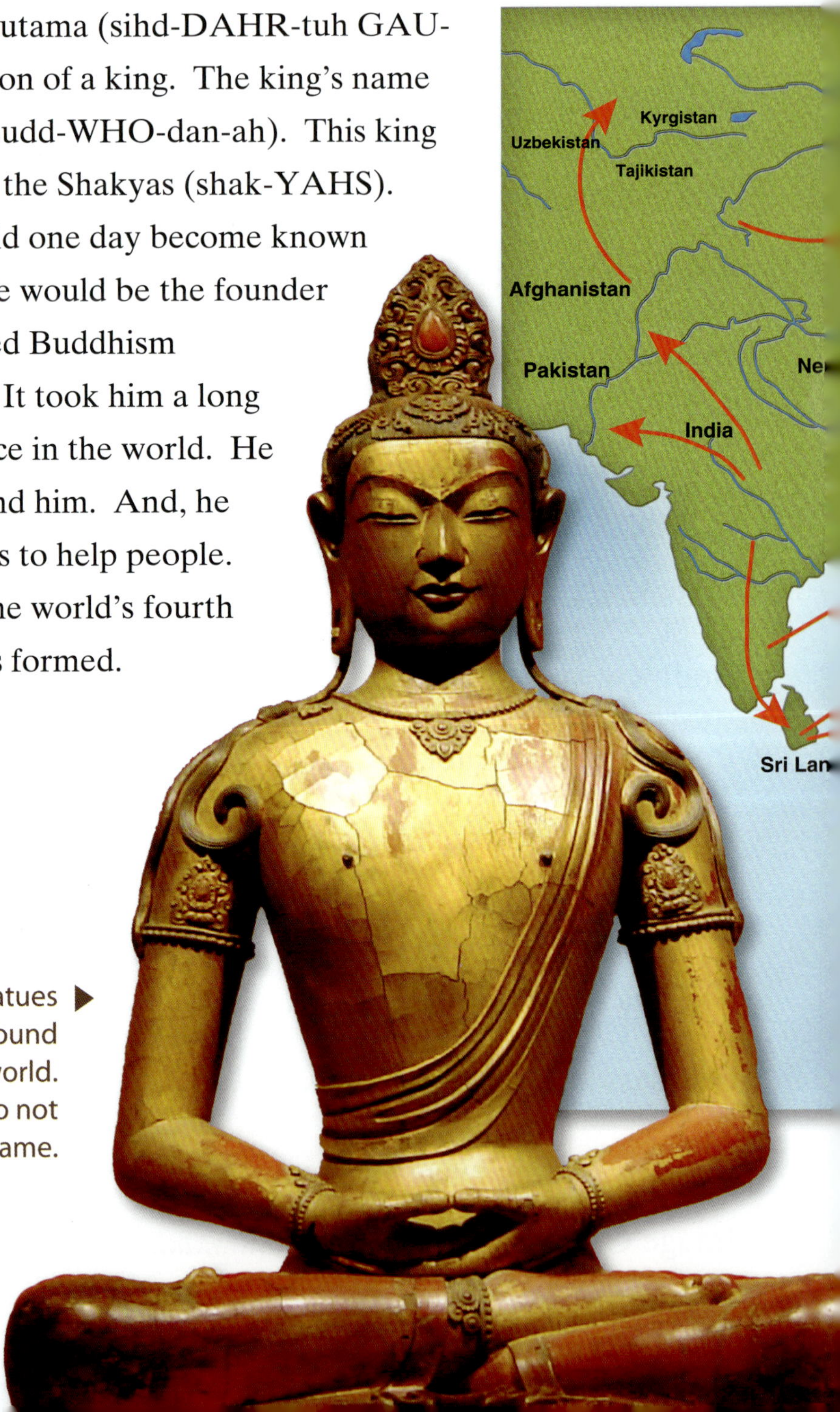

There are statues of Buddha found all over the world. And, they do not all look the same.

▲ Buddhism started in India. It spread north and to the other Asian countries.

Place in the World

Today, there are more than 325 million Buddhists around the world. Even though Buddhism began in India, it is the biggest major religion today in Japan, China, and Korea.

Many Buddhists

Since Buddhism began, thousands of different ways to practice the religion have been created. Only a small number of Buddhists today practice just as Buddha did.

History of India

The earliest Indian people lived in the south and central parts of the country. They were called Dravidians (druh-VID-ee-uhnz). The second group of early **settlers** came to the Indus Valley. These **tribes** came from central Europe and Asia. They were known as Aryans (AH-ree-uhz). This group of people lived in the Indus Valley for more than 1,000 years.

King Suddhodana's tribe lived in the north-central part of India. The Aryan people ruled the area where the family lived. But, the tribe ruled itself because it had a special agreement with the Aryan rulers.

▼ Indus River Valley

Patna today

Old City, New City

The Mauryas built their capital in what is present-day Patna. Patna is located in the northern part of India. It is close to the country of Nepal.

Writing Sanskrit

The Aryans developed a language. It was called Sanskrit (SAN-skruht). This is one of the oldest languages in the world.

Starting in 500 B.C., other cultures invaded India. However, the Indian people had the most powerful leaders. The Mauryan (MOR-yuhn) Empire was very powerful for about 140 years. The Gupta (GOOP-tuh) Empire was in control from A.D. 319–550.

This shows the style of the Dravidians.

The Astrologer

When Gautama was born, an **astrologer** (uh-STRAWL-uh-juhr) made a prediction. The prediction was that he would be either a great king or a monk. And, if he became a monk, he would leave his rich life behind to save **humanity** (hyu-MAN-uh-tee).

◀ Prince Gautama sees an old man and a sick man.

▼ Gautama sees a dead man.

King Suddhodana knew that if his son became a monk, he would leave home. The king did not want to lose his son. The king asked the astrologer what would cause Gautama to leave. The astrologer said that if Gautama saw an old man, a sick man, a dead man, and a monk, he would become religious. The king decided that he would do whatever he could to keep his son from leaving.

Born Special

Many stories about Gautama's birth say that he was able to talk and walk at birth. These stories are still told today and are believed by many people.

Gautama's Birthplace Today

Lumbini is a small town located near the Nepal-India border. This is where Gautama was born in 556 B.C. People from all over the world visit his birthplace each year.

◀ Finally, Gautama sees a monk.

Keeping the World Away

There was a lot of **poverty** (PAWV-uhr-tee) near where Gautama's family lived. So, the king did not let the prince see the outside world. The king was very wealthy. He did his best to keep his son away from the signs that would lead him to enter a religious life. He tried to make his son see only beauty and health.

King Suddhodana tried to keep his son from seeing people suffer. The young prince spent all his time in the three palaces that belonged to the family. For years, he did not see anything that normal people saw.

▼ Leaders of India today still live in large palaces.

◀ The *om* is an important symbol of Hinduism.

Early Religion

A popular religion in India during Gautama's time was Brahminism (BRAW-muh-nih-zuhm). Brahmins believed in a god named Brahma and other gods beneath him. That religion grew into Hinduism (HIN-doo-ih-zuhm). Hinduism is the largest religion in India today.

Art showing Brahma ▶

Guards were posted around the palaces. They kept him from making contact with people from the outside.

The homes where he stayed had beautiful gardens. There were many fountains. Music and dancing were all around him. Beautiful women lived on the grounds as well. Gautama's father wanted him to get used to comfort and beauty. King Suddhodana thought this would make the prince become a king and not a monk.

Hindus in India

Today, eight of every ten people in India are Hindu.

Looking Outside

Gautama grew up to be a strong young man. At that time, Indian society was defined by the **caste system**. This was a system that people were born into. It told people who they could marry. It controlled all parts of their lives. When he was 16 years old, Gautama married a princess from a nearby kingdom.

▼ This family of Brahmins were from the top caste level.

Indian wedding ceremonies include special traditions.

Gautama's life was very comfortable. But in time, he became restless. He was curious about the world beyond the palace walls. Gautama wanted to see his land and people.

The king knew he could not keep his son inside any longer. He made careful plans for Gautama's first trip into the streets of India. The king told the guards to make sure Gautama did not see any sick, old, or religious people on the trip.

Old System in Modern Times

The caste system officially ended in India in 1950. However, the caste system still has an impact today on whom Indians marry. Many people will not marry someone outside their own caste.

Beyond the Palace Walls

▲ Prince Gautama sees a sick man.

Gautama was led through the city. His guards stayed close by his side. He saw a few old men as he traveled. Gautama was confused. He had never seen old men before. He chased after them to find out who they were.

When he found them, he saw some people who were very sick. He also saw a funeral by the side of a river. For the first time in his life, Gautama saw death.

Gautama asked a friend what this all meant. The friend told him that all people get old eventually. Everyone gets sick at some time in life. And, in time, people die.

Gautama was upset by what he saw in the streets of India. He now knew that he would become old one day. And, he would become sick and die, also. After his trip through the streets, Gautama met a monk who was very calm. Gautama wanted to learn what the monk knew. He wanted to help find a way to end human suffering.

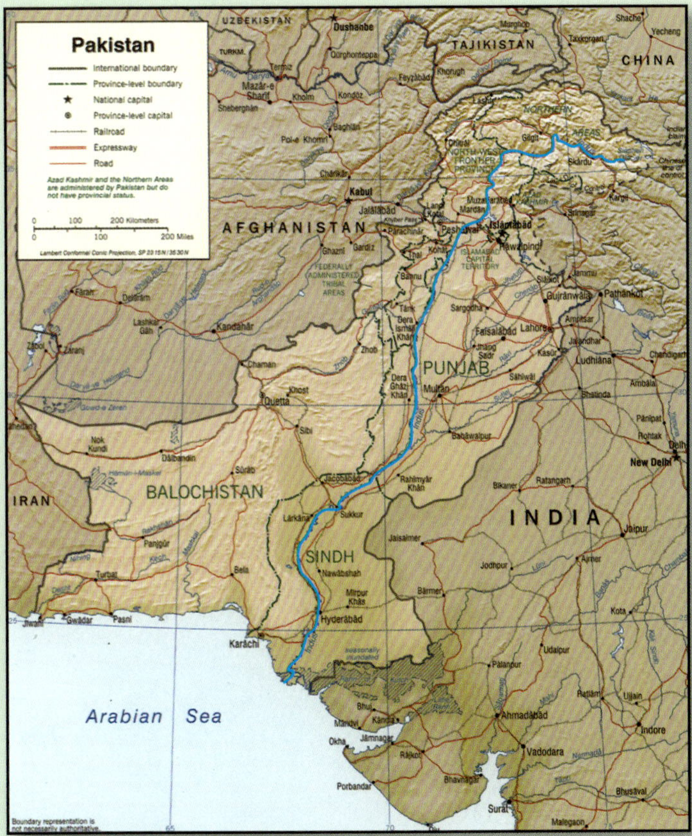

▲ The Indus River is now part of Pakistan.

Old World

India is the oldest living culture in the world. It is at least 10,000 years old. The name *India* came from the Indus River. The valleys around the river were the homes of the early settlers of India.

Violent History

India has fought in many wars. Different families have ruled over the land. It seems that India is too big and complex for any one group to rule it for long.

Goodbye to Comfort

Gautama decided to give up all his earthly belongings. Many religious people in India were doing this. They believed that this was a way to become more **spiritual** (SPIR-ih-chuh-wuhl).

Gautama decided he had to leave his home forever. He was 29 years old. He wanted to discover how to let go of suffering. He also wanted to help other people do the same.

By this time, Gautama and his wife had a baby boy. One day he kissed his wife and son as they slept. Then, he left the palace.

Gautama gave away his expensive clothing. Instead, he wore yellow monk's robes. He cut his long hair and shaved his head. The prince was shocked by how much suffering he saw around him. He left all the comforts of his rich life and went out alone to find truth.

Gautama leaves his wife and son.

Religious Leader

In the Indian religions, the **monk** is the religious leader and teacher. Gautama became a monk at this point in his life.

Desire

Gautama believed that humans suffer because they have desires. He tried to get rid of the desires he had in his life. He simplified his life as much as he could.

Some monks today still wear robes and shave their heads.

In Search of Truth

Gautama visited the great religious teachers in India at that time. He learned all they had to teach him. He felt that they did not have the answers he needed. So, he continued to search.

In India, it was common for certain religious people to eat very little food. Gautama ate and drank very little for six years. He spent a lot of time in **meditation** (med-uh-TAY-shuhn). The answers he needed did not come to him, so he tried harder.

He stopped drinking and eating completely. This was called **fasting**. He hoped that this would bring him the answers he needed. Instead, he almost died.

▲ This monk is meditating in a forest.

Gautama finally realized that the answers he was looking for were not coming to him by starving himself. It only made his body very weak. He realized that he needed to find a middle way. He would not live with too much comfort. He would also not live without the things he needed. Gautama would find a place in between the two.

◀ Gautama meditating

Fasting

In many religions, fasting is part of the customs. Gautama may have eaten as little as a grain of rice and a sesame seed each day. He got way too thin. He lost so much strength, he could not do anything anymore.

The Middle Way

Buddha called his teachings the "Middle Way." In other words, you need to find a happy medium. You cannot be successful at one extreme or the other.

Bodh Gaya

Gautama sat under a fig tree in the town of Bodh Gaya (BAWD GUY-aw). This town is in the Ganges (GAN-jeez) Valley of India. He wanted to find a way to end the suffering of all people. He decided to stay sitting under the tree until the answers came to him. He sat for many days.

At first he sat to clear his mind. Then, he sat in meditation. This helped him to see what he came to know as the truth. He knew the truth by looking into himself. He called this state **nirvana** (nir-VAW-nuh). It means that he was

unaware of everyone else. He was totally focused on his meditation.

From that time on, Gautama came to be known as "The Buddha." This means "he who is awake." He was 35 years old when this happened.

Snuffed Out

The word *nirvana* means "snuffed out." To Buddhists, this means that they forget about themselves.

Reaching Nirvana

Buddhists believe that the first step to reaching the state of nirvana is to do good for other people.

This temple is located in Bodh Gaya. ▶

▼ This is the tree under which Buddha meditated.

Becoming a Teacher

Buddha stayed under the tree for many more days. He finally had the answers that he had been searching for. Buddha decided to spend the rest of his life teaching other people what he learned.

He gave his first talk in an Indian town called Sarnath (SAHR-nahth). He spoke at a place called Deer Park. He explained what he

◀ This statue shows Buddha meditating.

had learned over the years. He spoke of something he called the Four Noble Truths. He also described the Eightfold Path. These are the basic beliefs of Buddhism.

THE EIGHTFOLD PATH

Wisdom	Ethical Conduct	Mental Development
• Right View	• Right Speech	• Right Effort
• Right Intention	• Right Action	• Right Mindfulness
	• Right Livelihood	• Right Concentration

FOUR NOBLE TRUTHS

- Life means suffering.
- The origin of suffering is attachment.
- The end of suffering is attainable.
- The path is the way out of suffering.

◀ This is Deer Park in Sarnath today.

Growing Bodhi

The bodhi tree under which Buddha sat has been destroyed many times since he died. It regrows every time and can still be seen today.

Bodhi Tree

Bodhi tree means tree of wisdom.

Buddhism Grows

The people who listened to his Sarnath talk were his first followers. They became the first Buddhist monks. This was the beginning of monk communities.

King Bimbisara (bim-buh-SAH-rah) ruled Magadha (MU-gaw-duh). This was the largest region in India at the time. The king heard Buddha's teachings. He gave Buddha a **monastery** (MAWN-uhs-ter-ee) to use. It was located in the capital of Magadha.

This was a place where Buddha and his followers could practice their beliefs during the rainy season in India. The king's gift allowed Buddhists to practice their beliefs throughout the years. It also gave many more people a chance to hear the teachings of the Buddha.

Ruins of the monasteries at Sarnath ▼

Buddha preaching to his first students

Monasteries from Long Ago

At Sarnath today, there are the remains of monasteries. These remains tell us that there were communities of monks in the area thousands of years ago.

Big Break

Buddhism became more widespread throughout India after King Ashoka (ah-SHOW-kuh) converted to Buddhism. This happened in the third century. He sent people to talk about Buddhism all over the world.

This is called the Ashoka pillar. The three-headed lion is a symbol of India today.

Everyone Is Welcome

Over time, Buddha's family found him. Buddha's son became a monk. His aunt and wife asked to become monks, too. At that time in India, women were not allowed to do this. People believed that women would make the community weak. Buddha did not agree. He made his wife and aunt the first Buddhist **nuns**.

The Buddha said that a person's place in the world did not matter. It did not matter how much money he or she had or where he or she came from. This belief was very different from that of the caste system, which had been so important in India.

Buddha believed all people could find truth. Everyone was welcome to follow his teachings.

This is a Buddhist temple in Hawaii.

Buddhism in America

There are over 1,000 Buddhist temples and Buddhist centers around the United States.

Showing Respect

A Buddhist temple is called a *vihara* (vih-HAWR-uh). When someone enters a *vihara*, he or she must remove his or her shoes to show respect for Buddha.

This is a shrine inside a Buddhist temple.

Buddha's Last Days

Buddha is honored in many ways. Here, his face is carved into a bodhi tree.

Buddha traveled around northern India for another 45 years. He taught anyone who wanted to listen to his message. Many thousands of people followed Buddha and listened to his words.

In his late 70s, his health began to fail him. When he was 80 years old, he told his friends and family he would be leaving them soon. He traveled to a small town where he died under a tree. Buddha did not choose another Buddhist leader to take his place. He felt that his teachings and rules would carry on the Buddhist **traditions** on their own.

Ancient Language

Many of the early Buddhist teachings are in an ancient language called Pali (PAW-lee).

Sharing Holidays

There are many types of Buddhists in the world today. Although the different types of Buddhism celebrate different holidays, all celebrate Buddha's birthday. All Buddhists also celebrate the day he reached nirvana.

▼ Buddhist monks celebrating Buddha's birthday.

Glossary

astrologer—someone who studies the position of the stars and planets and believes they affect people's lives

caste system—a social system in which class is decided by a person's family

fasting—to stop eating and drinking completely

humanity—all human beings as a group

meditation—sitting quietly and planning within the mind

monastery—a place where a community of people, especially monks, live religious lives

monk—a man who is a member of a religious group; lives with other monks

nirvana—state of being totally focused on meditation

nuns—women who belong to a religious group and have made promises to serve the religion

poverty—the state of having little or no money

settlers—a person who moves to and lives in a new country or area

spiritual—focusing on the soul or spirit instead of the physical being

traditions—the passing down of a culture from one age group to the next, especially through talking

tribes—groups of people brought together by having the same ancestors, customs, traditions, and leaders

Index

Image Credits

cover Corbis; p.1 Corbis; p.4 Jan Kovalcik/Shutterstock, Inc.; p. 5 Teacher Created Materials; p.6 Tibor Bognar/Alamy; p.7 (top) V. Muthuraman/SuperStock; p.7 (bottom) Corel; p.8 The Granger Collection, New York; pp.8–9 Book Matrix; p.9 Book Matrix; p.10 age fotostock/SuperStock; p.11 (top) iconex/Shutterstock, Inc.; p.11 (bottom) iStockphoto.com/Hector Joseph Lumang; p.12 Hulton-Deutsch Collection/Corbis; p.13 Cindy Hughes/Shutterstock, Inc.; p.14 The Granger Collection, New York; p.15 The Library of Congress; pp.16–17 Kurt De Bruyn/Shutterstock, Inc.; p.17 The Granger Collection, New York; p.18 Tan, Kim Pin/Shutterstock, Inc.; p.19 (top) James R. Hearn/Shutterstock, Inc.; p.19 (bottom) Vincent Hor/Shutterstock, Inc.; p.20 Tom Schmucker/Shutterstock, Inc.; pp.20–21 Robert Nickelsberg/Getty Images; p.21 Neil Cooper/Alamy; p.22 Public Domain; p.23 Ange/Alamy; pp.24–25 Maciej Wojtkowiak/Alamy; p.25 (top) Taolmor/Shutterstock, Inc.; p.25 (bottom) iStockphoto.com/Eromaze; p.26 World Religions Photo Library/Alamy; p.27 (top) Lisa Hoang/Shutterstock, Inc.; p.27 (bottom) Robert O. Brown Photography/Shutterstock, Inc.; p.28 Vladimir Pomortzeff/Shutterstock, Inc.; p.29 Gina Smith/Shutterstock, Inc.; back cover Pigscanfly/Dreamstime.com